HOW DID WE GET
the BIBLE?

HOW DID WE GET
the BIBLE ?

Tracy Macon Sumner

BARBOUR
PUBLISHING

Published by Barbour Publishing, Inc., P.O. Box 719, Uhrichsville, Ohio 44683 www.barbourbooks.com

Our mission is to publish and distribute inspirational products offering exceptional value and biblical encouragement to the masses.

Member of the
Evangelical Christian
Publishers Association

Printed in the United States of America.

Contents

Contents

Preface

If you're a Bible-believing Christian, you no doubt know that the Bible is no ordinary book. It is the very Word of God Himself, which He spoke and then had recorded, protected, preserved, and compiled for the benefit of His people. As such, you can know that every word of the Bible is truth; that you can count on it as your guide for your life of faith; and that God will make good on every promise recorded in its pages.

But how did He do it? How did God inspire people and arrange events so that the words He spoke through His Holy Spirit were accurately recorded and compiled, then preserved and passed down from generation to generation throughout the centuries?

The word *amazing* doesn't begin to describe the process God used to give us His written Word. From the time the actual writing began, some thirty-five centuries ago, until now, God has miraculously used imperfect people to give the world the one perfect book. God gave people—people He specifically chose to do the work of bringing forth the books of the Bible—the words He wanted them to write, then set in motion the events that led to the compilation and translation of the sixty-six books we have in the Bible today.

Though a book that lays out all the details of how we got the Bible could easily run to thousands of pages and include hundreds of names, dates, and events, this little book gives the reader a briefer, more concise overview of the people God used and the events He ordained to give us the most important book ever written.

This book will first give you snapshot accounts of the men (and possibly a woman or two) that God used to record His written Word. From there, it will tell you how He protected and preserved that written Word, moved people to compile the books we have in our Bible today, and made provision for us to have available a printed copy of that Word in our own language.

Most Christians have at least a basic grasp of the message of salvation that is presented throughout the Bible. Most also have some knowledge of the stories contained in its pages: from the story of Adam and Eve, to the account of Israel's exodus from Egypt, to the eyewitness testimonies of those who saw the deeds and heard the acts of Jesus Christ during His earthly ministry, to the men Jesus chose to spread His gospel message throughout the world. Comparatively few, however, understand how the stories, promises, warnings, and encouragements contained in the Bible came to be recorded for us to read today.

As you read through this book— even if you have a good grasp of the actual contents of the Bible—you may find yourself saying, "I hadn't thought of that before!" But God did! Looking forward from eternity past, He knew His

people would need the Bible as their
handbook for a life of faith, and He did
everything necessary to make sure we,
as well as believers before us and after
us, could have access to everything He
has to say about a victorious, growing
life of faith in Him.

1
God's Transmitters
The People Who Wrote the Bible

Take a look for a minute at your personal Bible. Have you ever wondered who was responsible for recording all the wonderful stories, promises, commands, and words of encouragement found in every book and on every page? Did God just drop them into someone's hand and say, "There's your Bible!"? Or did a bunch of people who lived long ago just sit around thinking about God and the things He had said and done and then just start writing?

The real story of how we got the books of the Bible is actually a lot more complex—and fascinating—than that. And it's also a lot more inspiring, for it demonstrates how God used ordinary,

fallible people—people just like us today—to give us His infallible written
Word. More on those people later, but
first let's take a look at *how* God used
these people to do what no one could
have done on his or her own.

More than forty men (and possibly a few women) wrote the books
we have in our Bible today. They came
from a wide variety of backgrounds
and vocations. In the Old Testament,
for example, Moses was a shepherd,
David a warrior and king, Ezra a priest,
Isaiah (and other writers of the Bible's
"prophetic" books) a prophet of God,
and Amos a fig farmer. The same kind
of variety can be found among the
New Testament writers. Matthew was
a tax collector, Peter and John were
fishermen, Luke was a physician and
historian, and the apostle Paul was a
tent maker and a devout Jewish religious leader.

Because we are imperfect people
who live with other imperfect people,

we know how hard it is to get three people—never mind more than forty—to agree on anything, let alone present consistent communication on a given subject. But the Bible never strays from its message, never contradicts itself, and always presents God's plan of redemption for humankind with perfect consistency.

But how did such a diverse group of writers—most of whom never met one another—pull that off?

The answer lies in the word *inspiration*.

When God Spoke, These People Listened—and Wrote!

As the apostle Paul declares, "All Scripture is given by inspiration of God" (2 Timothy 3:16). Most of us have a pretty good idea what it means to be inspired to do, say, or write something. Most every artist, poet, musician, or novelist can point to his or her own work and tell you exactly what inspired him or her to do it. Emotions such as love, anger, hatred, or grief have inspired artistic types throughout the centuries.

But in the context of scripture, the word *inspiration* means more than receiving an idea or an inkling of what to say or write. It means more than seeing a need for a particular message and writing it down. It means that God, through His Holy Spirit, spoke through a person and gave him or her His very own words to record. In short, the people who wrote the books of the Bible were instruments that God miraculously used—pencils in His hand, as someone once put it—to give us His written Word, the Bible.

That is precisely why some translations of the Bible render 2 Timothy 3:16 more literally, telling us that all scripture is "God-breathed," which means that God Himself spoke the words you read in the pages of your Bible today.

The apostle Peter, who was with Jesus during His earthly ministry, expounds on the truth that the Bible is the inspired Word of God when he writes, "No prophecy of Scripture is of any private interpretation, for prophecy never came by the will of man, but holy men of God spoke as they were moved by the Holy Spirit" (2 Peter 1:20–21).

Although the Bible was written by dozens of fallible human individuals from greatly diverse walks of life, it has one ultimate Author, and that's God Himself. The Bible is both the history of God's interactions with His people and the rest of the world, and His instruction manual for living a life that pleases Him—also known as a life of faith.

That's why you can count on the Bible as your ultimate source for everything you need to know to live a life of true faith and obedience to the author and finisher of that faith (see Hebrews 12:2).

How It All Started—
the Old Testament

The Old Testament traces the story of how humankind got its start; how sin corrupted a once-perfect creation; and how God set in motion the events, and prepared the people He used, to send Jesus Christ to redeem a fallen, sinful world.

The Old Testament is chock-full of some of the most familiar characters and stories in the Bible (Adam and Eve in the Garden of Eden, Noah and his ark, Israel's exodus from Egypt, and Jonah's three days in the belly of a giant sea creature—just to name a few), but more importantly, it demonstrates the power and care of a God who was constantly busy working (both up front and behind the scenes) to make sure His plan for redemption was brought to completion.

Here are the people God used to record the events and promises found in the Old Testament:

Moses—Though the book of Genesis doesn't name an author, many centuries of tradition hold that it was written by Moses, God's chosen man to lead the people of Israel out of Egyptian captivity. Moses is also credited with writing Exodus (see Exodus 17:14, 24:4–7, 34:27), Leviticus, Deuteronomy, and Numbers. It has also been suggested that Moses recorded the book of Job, which is widely believed to be the oldest book in the Bible. He also wrote one of the Psalms.

Joshua—The book of Joshua also doesn't specifically identify its author, but Jewish tradition and most modern-day Bible scholars hold that Joshua, Moses' successor as leader of Israel and the man who led the people of Israel into the Promised Land, recorded *most* of the book himself (see Joshua 24:26). The latter part of the book was obviously written after his death.

Samuel—Tradition holds that the

prophet Samuel, the last of the judges who presided over the nation of Israel, authored the book of Judges. It is also possible, but not certain, that he wrote the book of Ruth and parts of 1 and 2 Samuel.

Ezra and Nehemiah—According to Jewish tradition, Ezra, who led a second wave of exiles back to Judah from the Babylonian Captivity (around 605–530 BC), wrote parts of the book that bears his name (though it is apparent from the tone of the book that he didn't write all of it), and also compiled and edited 1 and 2 Chronicles. Ezra or Nehemiah may have authored the book of Nehemiah, which is widely thought to be Nehemiah's autobiography.

The Book of Esther—Though this book doesn't name its author, the most popular and lasting tradition says that Mordecai, a major character in the story, recorded the book, which gives the account of heroism in the face of a threatened genocide against the Hebrew people. Another possible author is Nehemiah.

The Book of Job—As mentioned earlier, Moses may have written the book of Job, which is the account of the suffering of a righteous man who had done nothing to deserve it. Other possible authors are King Solomon or Job himself.

Psalm Writers

It is commonly—and wrongly—thought that David wrote the entire book of Psalms, but biblical scholars believe that at least twelve writers contributed to the book—seven of whom we know by name. Of the 150 psalms, 48 are not ascribed to an individual writer. David wrote at least 73 psalms, and it is likely that he penned some of the ones whose authors are, at least to us, unknown. Asaph, a

continued on next page. . .

---

continued from previous page. . .

music director during the reigns of kings David and Solomon, wrote a dozen psalms (50, 73–83), and another dozen are credited to the Sons of Korah, Levites who served in the temple (42–49, 84, 85, 87, 88). Solomon wrote two psalms that we know of (72, 127), but 1 Kings 4:29–32 says that he wrote many more. Hemen, who lived at the time of David and Asaph, wrote Psalm 88; and Ethan, who ministered with Asaph and Hemen in temple worship, wrote Psalm 89. Finally, from the "Did You Know?" department, Moses wrote Psalm 90, which is most likely the oldest of the psalms.

Solomon—Israel's third monarch, the son of King David, is widely credited with writing the first twenty-nine chapters of Proverbs (Agur wrote Proverbs 30, and Lemuel wrote Proverbs 31), as well as Ecclesiastes and the Song of Solomon. His writings contain excellent examples of godly wisdom, as well as encouragements to remain in the faith.

Isaiah—Isaiah, the son of Amoz, who ministered to the people of Judah through the reigns of four different kings, recorded his own book of prophecies, which is the Old Testament book most often quoted in the New Testament. Isaiah prophesied from the time of King Uzziah (around 740 BC) to the time of King Hezekiah (around 681 BC). Isaiah's message is one of God's intolerance of sin, of judgment for that sin, and of hope, for the Messiah is coming to provide atonement for the sin of humankind.

Jeremiah—The "weeping prophet," so called because of the mournful tone of his prophecies concerning the coming destruction of Jerusalem, penned the book of prophecies that bears his name and the companion book of Lamentations. He is also believed, according to Jewish tradition, and according to many biblical scholars, to have recorded 1 Kings and 2 Kings. Jeremiah's prophecies cover the dark period of time in Judah's history from the thirteenth year of the reign of King Josiah (627 BC) until several years after the Babylonian invasion (586 BC), which he foretold.

Ezekiel—The prophet and priest Ezekiel ministered to the people of Judah just before and during the Babylonian Captivity, recording his prophecies in the book that bears his name. Ezekiel's prophetic book is seen as a companion piece to that of Jeremiah, but Ezekiel focuses more on God's message of restoration for His people once they repent of their sin.

Daniel—Daniel, who is never referred to as a prophet in his book, recorded his life experiences and prophecies, which cover a time during and shortly after the Babylonian Captivity. Daniel's prophecies foretold the coming of several key historic figures, such as Alexander the Great, Cleopatra, and most importantly, Jesus Christ. They also foretell the coming of the Antichrist, as well as the second coming of Jesus Christ at the end of days.

The "Minor" Prophets—Don't let the term "minor prophet" fool you. These twelve Old Testament prophets recorded books containing shorter (but still important) "God-breathed" prophecies for different times and different groups throughout the history of Israel:

- **Hosea**—Hosea was a prophet of God who lived and served in Israel around the time of the reigns of kings Uzziah, Jotham, Ahaz, and Hezekiah of Judah, and Jeroboam of Israel. God commanded Hosea to marry a prostitute named

Gomer, as an illustration of both the waywardness of God's people and of His never-ending love for them and willingness to do what it took to "win" them back.

- **Joel**—This prophet, identified as "the son of Pethuel" (Joel 1:1), was a well-educated man who knew the words of the earlier prophets, and who used an invasion of locusts (figurative or literal) on Judah to illustrate a coming judgment, specifically against Jerusalem, if the people didn't awaken from their spiritual lethargy. The historic context of Joel's prophecy isn't certain, but it is believed he wrote during the reign of King Joash (835–796 BC).

- **Amos**—This farmer-turned-prophet from the town of Tekoa in Judah prophesied to Israel and Judah, as well as surrounding nations, during the reign of King Uzziah of Judah and King Jeroboam II of Israel. This was a time of prosperity in Israel, but also a time of deep spiritual malaise. Amos's prophecies pronounce judgment for that malaise, but they also express hope for those who wholeheartedly turn back to God.

- **Obadiah**—Obadiah wrote his prophecy—nineteen verses in a single chapter, the shortest book in the Old Testament—which foretells the destruction of Edom for its opposition to the nation of Israel (around 840 BC). Nothing is known of

Obadiah's personal history.

- **Jonah**—If the extent of your knowledge of the Bible is limited to what you heard in Sunday school as a child, you know that Jonah was the wayward prophet who ran from God and ended up spending three days in the belly of a giant sea creature. Jonah lived and served around the time of the reign of King Jeroboam II (around 760 BC). After God restored him, Jonah preached to the city of Nineveh, which repented and was spared destruction.

- **Micah**—A native of southern Judah, Micah prophesied during the reigns of kings Jotham, Ahaz, and Hezekiah (750–686 BC). His prophecies were against the

princes and people of Judah
for their abusive treatment
of the poor.

- **Nahum**—Nahum
  prophesied in the years
  around 660 BC, and his
  prophecies proclaim the
  fall of Nineveh, the same
  city that one hundred years
  earlier had repented at the
  preaching of Jonah and was
  spared. All that is known of
  Nahum's personal life is that
  he was born in a place called
  Elkosh (see Nahum 1:1).

- **Habakkuk**—The rebellious,
  hard-hearted nation of
  Judah was about to be
  invaded by the Babylonians.
  God told Habakkuk that
  this judgment was coming.
  Though Habakkuk didn't
  understand why God would
  use such evil people to
  judge His own people, he

acknowledged that God knew what He was doing—as well as the best way to do it.

- **Zephaniah**—A contemporary of Jeremiah's and the son of a man named Cushi (see Zephaniah 1:1), Zephaniah wrote of a coming judgment on the people of Israel, but he also wrote of God's promises of eventual restoration and salvation for His people.

- **Haggai**—The Jews had returned to Judah from the Babylonian Exile, and God had made their top priority the construction of a new temple to replace the old one, which the Babylonians destroyed seventy years earlier. Haggai's prophecies chided the people for not finishing what they had

started sixteen years earlier,
upon their return to their
homeland, and commanded
them to again get busy with
the work.

- **Zechariah**—Like Haggai,
  Zechariah, who identifies
  himself as "the son of
  Berechiah" (Zechariah
  1:1), focuses his writing on
  the need to complete the
  construction of the new
  temple in Jerusalem. The
  first eight chapters focus on
  the command to complete
  the project, the final six on
  the promises of blessing for
  doing so.

- **Malachi**—The Old
  Testament closes with
  the writings of the
  prophet Malachi, who
  was a contemporary of
  Nehemiah's. Malachi's
  prophecies chided the

people of Judah for falling
into the same kind of
sins that had led to the
destruction of Jerusalem
and the seven decades of
captivity in Babylon.

Some "New Covenant" Writing

The Bible as a whole is the story of God's plan for the redemption of humankind. The Old Testament is more or less the story of His "laying the groundwork" for bringing salvation to the world, and the New Testament tells the story of how God sent His Son, Jesus Christ, into the world to bring the news and do the work of that salvation (see John 3:16), and then what that gift means to individual believers.

Christianity Gets Its Start

If you want to learn all the Bible has to say about the life of Jesus Christ, and about the beginning of the Christian faith following Christ's death and resurrection, you'll find it in the first five books of the New Testament—the four Gospels and the book of Acts (also called the Acts of the Apostles).

Now take a moment to get to know some of the New Testament writers:

Matthew—Talk about a transformation! Here's a man who was part of the most hated class of people in first-century Israel—tax collectors for the Roman government, whom the Jewish people saw as the worst of sinners— but who heard and obeyed Jesus' call to follow Him (see Matthew 9:9; Luke 5:27–28) and later wrote the Gospel intended specifically for the first wave of Jewish believers.

Mark—Most scholars believe that the author of the Gospel of Mark was a young man named John Mark, who is mentioned by name in the book of Acts as a traveling companion of the apostles Paul and Barnabas (see Acts

12:25). It is also widely believed that the young man who fled the scene of Jesus' arrest in the Garden of Gethsemane naked (see Mark 14:51–52) was also John Mark.

Luke—Luke, a first-century historian, physician, and missionary who wrote the Gospel bearing his name, as well as the book of Acts, is unique among the writers of biblical books in that he is the only Gentile (non-Jew) to write a book of the Bible. It is believed that Luke accompanied Paul in his later missionary journeys, because he changes the narrative in Acts to include himself (see Acts 16:11). Luke's skill as a writer and historian are amply demonstrated in the book of Acts, as well as in his Gospel, which is the most detailed and historical of the four.

John—The apostle who refers to himself as the disciple "whom Jesus loved" (John 13:23) was a fisherman-turned-disciple who wrote the Gospel of John, as well as the three epistles bearing his name (1, 2, and 3 John) and the book of Revelation. Jesus referred to John and his brother James, the sons of a fisherman named Zebedee (see Matthew 4:21), as *Boanerges*, which means "Sons of Thunder" (Mark 3:17), the meaning of which isn't explained.

The Epistles:
Words to Live By!

If you're like most people, when you've finished reading the Gospels and the book of Acts, you will likely ask how you can practically apply what you've just read in your own walk of faith. You'll find answers in the next twenty-one books of the New Testament, which will give you practical commandments, guidelines, and promises for living the Christian life.

These "epistles"—or letters— were written to various individuals, churches, and groups of believers to encourage, challenge, and instruct them in the specifics of an individual's life of faith in Christ and of the basics of life within the church body.

There are five known writers of the New Testament epistles, including the apostle John. Here is the lowdown on the others:

Paul—Humanly speaking, if you were going to appoint someone as the "apostle to the Gentiles" (Romans 11:13; Ephesians 3:8) and as the human author of most of the books of the New Testament, it wouldn't be this guy. Paul (he was called Saul before his conversion) was a devout Jewish religious leader in first-century Jerusalem who spent a lot of his time persecuting the fledgling church (see 1 Timothy 1:13). But after a spectacular conversion experience on the road to Damascus (he was on his way to that city to cause more trouble for the church there), Paul spent the remainder of his life faithfully and passionately following God's call to preach the gospel of Christ to the non-Jewish world. He planted new churches in various cities around the region, and wrote letters to those churches that would later become an important part of the New Testament. Paul is known with certainty to have written the epistles of Romans, 1 and 2 Corinthians, Galatians, Ephesians, Philippians, Colossians, 1 and 2 Thessalonians, 1 and 2 Timothy, Titus, and Philemon. Some scholars believe he also wrote the epistle to the Hebrews, but differences in tone and style cast serious doubt on his authorship of that letter.

Who Wrote Hebrews?

The authorship of the book of Hebrews—the theme of which is the life, death, and resurrection of Jesus Christ, and how those events are related to Old Testament prophecies regarding the Jewish Messiah—remains

continued on next page. . .

continued from previous page. . .

a mystery to this day. Some have speculated that Hebrews was another of Paul's epistles, though it is in many ways different in structure and tone than Paul's other letters. One obvious difference between Hebrews and Paul's epistles is that Paul identifies himself as the writer in all thirteen of his epistles, and always in the first word of the letter. Others have suggested that Silas, Barnabas, Apollos, Luke, or Philip penned the book. It has even been suggested that Priscilla, the wife of Aquila, wrote Hebrews. If that were true, Priscilla would be the only female author of a New Testament book.

James—The New Testament mentions several men named James, but most scholars agree that the author of the epistle of James is "the Lord's brother" (Galatians 1:19; see also Mark 6:3), the son of Mary and Joseph.

Peter—Of the original twelve men Jesus called to be His apostles (see Matthew 4:18–20; Mark 1:16–18; Luke 5:1–11), none played a larger role in establishing the early church than Peter, the simple fisherman from the Sea of Galilee coastal town of Bethsaida, who received and followed Jesus' call to be His apostle to the Jews; who preached with power following Jesus' return to heaven (Acts 2:14–39); and who wrote the two epistles that bear his name. He was the brother of Andrew, another of the twelve apostles and the one who first introduced Peter to Jesus (John 1:40–42).

Jude—The authorship of the epistle of Jude is not certain, but Jude (or Judas) identifies himself as the brother of James (Jude 1). Though Jude doesn't identify himself as Jesus' earthly half brother, it is likely he was referring to

Jesus' half brother James as his own brother.

So Why *These* Books by *These* People?

All of the writings that make up what we know as the Old Testament were completed by around 500 BC, and all the books that make up the New Testament we have today were finished by the end of the first century AD.

But what some Christians don't know is that the books included in our Bible weren't the only ones written concerning the history of the Jewish people, concerning the life of Jesus Christ, or concerning the life of faith in Christ. That leaves several questions unanswered for the average Bible reader. For example, how do we know that the Bible we have today says the same things the writers wrote thousands of years ago? And why were the books we have in the Bible now included, while others were left out?

For the answers to these all-important questions, read chapter 2, which tells the story of how the truth of God's written Word has been preserved throughout the centuries. Then move on to chapter 3, which will tell you how we got what is called the "canon" of scripture.

2
Keeping the Bible
"On Message"
How God Has Preserved His Written Word

Just about any Bible-believing Christian who has had a chance to talk to a skeptic about God's written Word has probably heard objections to the accuracy of the scriptures as we have them today. "How can you say the Bible is accurate?" the doubter protests. "The first books in the Bible were written thousands of years ago, so how is it possible that they say the same thing they did when they were written?"

A good question indeed, and one for which God has provided the answer.

Speaking through the prophet

Isaiah, God told His people, "The grass withers, the flower fades, but the word of our God stands forever" (Isaiah 40:8). Jesus echoed the message behind those words when He told His disciples, "Heaven and earth will pass away, but My words will by no means pass away" (Matthew 24:35).

Obviously, God is passionately committed to doing whatever it takes to preserve His primary form of communication to His people, His written Word. And just as He used fallible men—men He called and equipped— to give humankind His words, He later used fallible men to preserve and care for His Word.

Caretakers of God's Written Word

If you have even the most basic understanding of how God does things, you know that more often than not, He uses people to do things He could just as easily—and most of the time more effectively—do Himself. That includes the task of preserving and protecting His written Word and perpetuating it from generation to generation.

After all, the Bible tells us, that was God's purpose for choosing the people of Israel.

In his letter to the Romans, the apostle Paul writes, "What advantage then has the Jew, or what is the profit of circumcision? Much in every way! Chiefly because to them were committed the oracles of God" (Romans 3:1–2). In other words, God granted the people of Israel—His chosen people, according to scripture—many privileges, but He also entrusted them with the high and holy purpose of taking care of scripture and passing it on to future generations.

This was certainly an awesome and solemn task, a fact reflected in God's command to Moses: "You shall not add to the word which I command you, nor take from it, that you may keep the commandments of the LORD your God which I command you" (Deuteronomy 4:2). In other words, those who were entrusted with caring for the Word of God had to do so with great care, making certain that every one of His commands and promises was preserved perfectly.

The Dead Sea Scrolls— Strong Evidence of Old Testament Accuracy

In 1947 a young Bedouin goat herder found some clay jars hidden away in a series of caves near the valley of the Dead Sea. Inside the jars were leather scrolls, the first of approximately one thousand documents discovered at Qumran between 1947 and 1979. These documents are the now-famous Dead Sea Scrolls.

continued on next page. . .

continued from previous page. . .

The writing on some of the scrolls showed that a commune of monastic farmers lived in the valley from about 150 BC until AD 70. But, more importantly, the Dead Sea Scrolls also included a complete copy of the book of Isaiah, another fragmented copy of Isaiah containing chapters 38–66 of that book, and fragments of almost every Old Testament book. Most of the fragments were from Isaiah and the Pentateuch (Genesis, Exodus, Leviticus, Numbers, and Deuteronomy). A frayed copy of the books of Samuel was also found, as well as two complete chapters of the book of Habakkuk.

The discovery of the Dead Sea Scrolls was considered one of the outstanding archaeological finds of the twentieth century,

continued on next page. . .

continued from previous page. . .

mostly because they included
the only known surviving copies of biblical text recorded
before AD 100. They are also
important to biblical scholars
because, apart from a few insignificant spelling changes
and other small differences, the
scrolls match the Hebrew text
that was the basis of today's Old
Testament.

Moses and the Levites

The first man charged with accurately
recording the words of God was Moses,
the man God chose to lead the people
of Israel out of Egyptian captivity and
slavery. Moses had a lot on his plate
in those days. In addition to receiving
and carrying out God's instructions for
leading the Israelites (an awesome task
for which God provided him help),
Moses also had to write down what

God said and everything that happened to him during those years (see Deuteronomy 31:24).

As Moses' death drew near, he entrusted the care and keeping of the Book of the Law (the first five books in the Bible) to the Levites, whose job it was to assist the priests of Israel. That included reading the books to the people of Israel every seven years (see Deuteronomy 31:9–13). Once Moses had completed his writing, he "commanded the Levites, who bore the ark of the covenant of the LORD, saying: 'Take this Book of the Law, and put it beside the ark of the covenant of the LORD your God' " (Deuteronomy 31:25–26).

From that time forward, as the Israelites took possession of the Promised Land, the Levites zealously carried out Moses' command to safeguard the scriptures. Eventually, however, that job fell into the hands of another group of men.

A Job Fit
for a King

Though God had intended that He Himself would be king over the nation of Israel, He knew that the people would soon turn away from Him and ask to be given a human king, just like the nations around them (see Deuteronomy 17:14–15; 1 Samuel 8:1–9). Though it was not part of God's plan that a human king should rule Israel, He still lovingly made provision for the preservation of His written Word during the monarchy.

When God gave Moses the Book of the Law and commanded him to record everything He had said, He included instructions that the kings of Israel were to follow regarding the books: "Also it shall be, when he sits on the throne of his kingdom, that he shall write for himself a copy of this law in a book, from the one before the priests, the Levites. And it shall be with him, and he shall read it all the days of his life, that he may learn to fear the LORD his God and be careful to observe all the words of this law and these statutes" (Deuteronomy 17:18–19).

God was so committed to preserving His law, and so committed to making sure the kings of Israel knew and obeyed it, that He commanded each man who would later serve as king—Saul, David, Solomon, and so on—to make a copy of it for himself, using the books the Levites had preserved, and then carefully read and obey it for the rest of his life.

Again, however, the work of preserving the Book of the Law was passed on to another group of men.

A New Era of Bible Preservation

In 586 BC the Babylonians, under the command of King Nebuchadnezzar, sacked Jerusalem, looted and destroyed the holy temple, and took many of the people living there away from their home to Babylon, where they stayed for the next seventy years. This part of Israel's history is called the Babylonian Captivity.

Up until the day the Babylonians attacked Jerusalem, the Israelites still kept a copy of the Book of the Law inside the ark of the covenant, which was stored inside the temple. And though the temple itself was leveled by the Babylonians, the temple scriptures were preserved.

During the Babylonian Captivity, certain Levites began copying the scriptures and distributing them to the other Israelites living in Babylon. These Levites came to be known as *scribes*, and they gained distinction among the people for their unsurpassed knowledge of the scriptures, as well as their accuracy in copying them.

The scribes followed a painstaking process, which had been developed over time since the beginning of the monarchy in Israel, for faithfully reproducing copies of the books of the Law. This was many centuries before the development of any kind of printing technology, so they had to do their work by hand. That they did, while following a detailed, meticulous set of rules and regulations, all of which ensured that the job was done with complete accuracy.

Following a Process

The Jewish scribes knew they weren't handling just any set of writings. These were the words of God Himself they were copying, and they approached their work with the diligence and passion due such an important calling. They also held fast to the rules for the transcribing, which is recorded in the Talmud, an ancient record of discussions pertaining to Jewish law, ethics, customs, and history.

Here is a quick overview of those rules:

- The scribe was required to prepare a parchment and dedicate it to the Lord before he began his work. The parchments would be clean, using the skins of only clean animals, both for writing on and binding the manuscripts.
- Each column on the parchment could include no fewer than forty-eight lines, and no more than sixty lines. Letters and words alike had to be spaced at a certain distance, and no word could touch another. This helped avoid confusion in reading as well as errors in future copying.
- The ink used in the process was always black and of a special mixture used only for copying scripture.

- Even when the scribe had memorized a passage of scripture by heart, he was not allowed to write it down from memory. He was still required to copy from an authentic copy of scripture; and as he wrote, he had to pronounce every word aloud.

- Every time the scribe wrote the Hebrew word for the name of God, he was required to wipe his pen clean and wash his entire body. This was in reverence for God and for His Word.

- After the copying was completed, the scroll was to be examined and checked for accuracy within thirty days. If the scribe made even one error, the entire sheet on which the mistake was made was destroyed. If mistakes were found on three separate

pages, the entire manuscript
was condemned.

- The scribe counted not just
  every word and paragraph
  in the manuscript, but every
  letter. Each paragraph, word,
  and letter had to correspond
  perfectly to the original.

Once the process of copying a manuscript was completed, the new copy could be stored only in sacred places, such as in a synagogue. No parchment containing the name of God could be destroyed, so when a copy became worn out and illegible in time, it was stored or buried in a *genizah*, which is a Hebrew word meaning a "hiding place," which was usually located in a synagogue or Jewish cemetery. This is why no original Old Testament manuscripts survive today.

This detailed and exacting process of copying and recopying the Hebrew scriptures in ancient times led to copies of the Old Testament that held incredibly true to their original words and intent. Some estimates hold that copies of the Old Testament text used in translating the Bible into English (see chapters 4 and 6) were 99.9 percent true to the original—with the only deviations being in updated spelling and punctuation.

Jesus and the Scribes

When you think of the word *scribe*, you might wonder if those were some of the same men Jesus often came into conflict with during His earthly ministry. In truth, the scribes who lived and worked during Jesus' earthly ministry—"teachers of the law," as He called them— did the same kind of work as the earlier generations of Jewish scribes.

In Matthew 23 alone, Jesus uses the phrase "woe to you

continued on next page...

continued from previous page. . .

scribes" at least seven times. These scribes were probably just as passionate in copying God's Word as were their predecessors, and they worked tirelessly to teach the people that same Word.

So why did Jesus have such a problem with these men?

First of all, the scribes were among the group of Jewish religious leaders who watched every move Jesus made and accused Him repeatedly of violating the law. They condemned Him for associating with sinners (Mark 2:16; Luke 5:30), charged Him with blasphemy for telling a man that his sins were forgiven (Mark 2:6–7), and watched to see if He would heal on the Sabbath so that they could accuse Him (Luke 6:7)—as well as many other

continued on next page. . .

continued from previous page. . .
incidents recorded in the Gospels.

Jesus knew that the scribes who opposed Him—though not all of them did; Nicodemus, who later became one of Jesus' followers, was a scribe (see John 3)—did so out of a legalistic spirit that allowed them to know what the scriptures said but without any understanding of what they really meant.

Preserving the Word
in the Christian Era

The Jewish scribes continued their work up to and after the time of Jesus' earthly ministry. That work continued even after the Roman destruction of Jerusalem in AD 70.

Eventually, the Masoretes, a line of Jewish scribes and scholars, took over the work of preserving the scriptures. Working between the sixth and eleventh centuries, these men used intricate number systems in their work and produced what is called the Masoretic Text, a highly accurate copy of the Old Testament text, which was the basis of most modern Bible translations.

While the work the scribes and Masoretes performed ensured that the Old Testament texts were preserved to perfection, God used other means to preserve the books of the New Testament.

New Testament Preservation

Bible skeptics often claim that the New Testament was written so long after the events depicted in the Gospels and the book of Acts that there is no way they can be considered reliable. They further hold that the content of all New Testament books has been copied and recopied so many times—

by hand, no less—that the content has become degraded to the point where we can't know for certain exactly what the New Testament writers originally recorded.

The facts, however, don't support that kind of skepticism. On the contrary, they demonstrate the blessed truth that God worked through men to preserve not only the Old Testament, but the New Testament as well.

As of today, thousands—estimates range between four thousand and six thousand—of handwritten copies of the Greek New Testament have been discovered, as well as thousands more in other languages. Some of these manuscripts are complete Bibles, and others are complete books or pages. The oldest of the fragments—many of which are in museums around the world, including many in Europe and North America—date back as far as AD 130, with many others dated between the second and sixteenth centuries.

There is a wealth of ancient New Testament manuscripts and fragments available today, but the all-important question of our time is this: How close are they in content to our modern-day Bibles? Obviously, language has changed greatly over the past two thousand years, but has the actual content of the New Testament been changed in any significant way?

Experts who have studied the ancient New Testament manuscripts tell us that there are tens of thousands of variants found between them—and, of course, between those manuscripts and the New Testament we have today. However, the vast majority of those variations are relatively insignificant changes, such as misspellings, updated spellings, syntax, and other minor variants that have no effect on the actual content. Of the remaining variations, only five have been found to cast any doubt at all on the accuracy of the text. (If you carefully examine your own

Bible, you'll probably find footnotes regarding five "questionable" passages: Mark 16:9–20; Luke 22:20, 43–44, 23:34; and John 7:53–8:11.)

Furthermore, the early church fathers—well-known Christian leaders from the second and third centuries of the Christian era—quoted the New Testament extensively in their writings, so extensively that, according to some scholars, all but eleven New Testament verses appear somewhere in their writings. In other words, it is nearly possible to reconstruct the *entire* New Testament from the church fathers' writings alone!

The bottom line, most Bible scholars tell us, is that most translations today contain essentially the same content as the first-century originals. In other words, the New Testament we have today is the same one written nearly two thousand years ago.

3
Why *These* Books?
The Compilation of the
Canon of Scripture

Writing to a young pastor named Timothy, the apostle Paul makes an important statement: "*All* Scripture is given by inspiration of God, and is profitable for doctrine, for reproof, for correction, for instruction in righteousness, that the man of God may be complete, thoroughly equipped for every good work" (2 Timothy 3:16–17, italics added).

This passage points out two very important facts about the Word of God. First, that God has "inspired" *all* scripture. In chapter one you read that the word *inspired* as it is used in this verse means that God, through the Holy Spirit, spoke His own words through the human writers of scripture.

Second, Paul communicated to Timothy that he, as well as every other believer past and present, could depend on the words of scripture as being the promises and warnings, the instructions and guidelines, that God has given to show believers how to live a growing, victorious life of faith.

But how can we know for certain that every word of every book in the Bible is indeed "inspired" and therefore "profitable for doctrine, reproof, for correction, for instruction in righteousness"?

At the time the canon of scripture—meaning the list of books considered "inspired" and authoritative, the books that met God's perfect standard—was established, there were many, many letters and "Gospels" making their way around what was then the Christian world. But nowhere in the Bible does God tell us specifically which books He intended to be part of His written Word.

So how do we know that the books of our Bible are the right ones? The answer lies in the great care God put into making sure all the words He inspired the biblical writers to record were kept in the blessed book He has prepared and given us.

That work, of course, began with the Old Testament.

The Hebrew Canon of Scripture

The Hebrew scriptures—also known as the Old Testament—were written from the time period from about 1400 BC through around 400 BC, when the prophet Malachi recorded his book. All of these books were written in Hebrew and passed down from generation to generation of Jewish people, who from the time of their writing accepted them as the authentic, inspired Word of God.

Between 400 BC and the birth of Christ, several other books—known as the Apocrypha (see sidebar)—made their way into Jewish popular culture. But while the vast majority of Jews didn't accept these books as scripture, most valued these works as good literary sources of history and some spiritual insight.

By the time of Jesus' birth, the canon of Hebrew scripture was pretty much decided. The Jews recognized that Moses, the prophets, and other writers were God's messengers and therefore accepted their work as the inspired Word of God. About AD 90, Jewish elders met at the council at Jamnia (in Judea, near the Mediterranean coast) and affirmed the Hebrew canon, at the same time rejecting the books of the Apocrypha as scripture.

Around AD 95, Flavius Josephus, a Jewish historian and priest, recognized the Hebrew canon as the books now included in the Old Testament. (Like the council at Jamnia, he listed just twenty-two books, not thirty-nine, but that can be accounted for by the way books were kept in ancient times.)

By the mid-third century, the church was in almost complete agreement about the Hebrew canon of scripture—which is underscored by the fact that nowhere in the New Testament is any book outside the accepted Hebrew canon quoted, whereas the Old Testament is quoted extensively. There was, however, some debate about the books of the Apocrypha, which to this day are still included in some Roman Catholic Bibles but are not considered part of the canon in Protestant circles.

What about
the Apocrypha?

If you've had a chance to peruse a Roman Catholic Bible, you may notice that it contains several more Old Testament books than most Protestant Bibles. These extra books make up what is referred to as the Apocrypha, which means "hidden." These books, as well as additions to the books of Esther and Daniel, were written mostly in the years between the writing of Malachi, the last Old Testament book (approximately 400 BC), and the birth of Jesus Christ. The books in the Apocrypha are as follows: 1 Esdras, 2 Esdras, Tobit, Judith, Wisdom of Solomon, Ecclesiasticus, Baruch, the Letter of Jeremiah, Prayer of Manasseh, 1 Maccabees, and 2 Maccabees.

The Jewish people had

continued on next page. . .

continued from previous page. . .

great respect for the books of the Apocrypha but never accepted them as part of the Hebrew (Old Testament) canon. Likewise, few first- or second-century Christians believed those books belonged in the canon of scripture—as evidenced by the fact that the New Testament quotes the Old Testament many times, but never mentions anything from the Apocryphal books.

Though there are many errors and contradictions in the Apocrypha, some of the books provide excellent extra-biblical historical information. For example, 1 Maccabees and 2 Maccabees tell the story of a Jewish national liberation movement during the second century BC that won the Jews their independence from the

continued on next page. . .

> *continued from previous page. . .*
> Seleucid king Antiochus IV Epiphanes, whose repression of the Jews and their religious practices sparked the violent revolt.

Even after the books of the Hebrew canon were completed, God was far from finished communicating with His people—and far from finished overseeing the complete list of books He wanted in His Bible.

Many Were Written, but Few Were Chosen

By the end of the first century of the Christian era, every book of what would later be known as the New Testament was completed. At least eight different people (depending on who wrote Hebrews) received the God-given words they recorded for the various churches and individuals to whom they ministered.

But the evidence points out that these people also produced other writings, most of which have long since been lost. For example, 1 Corinthians 5:9 tells us that the apostle Paul had written an earlier letter to the Corinthian church. Knowing that, it's hard to imagine that Paul, Peter, James, Matthew, and other New Testament writers didn't produce other writings not now included in the New Testament.

In addition to the "extra-biblical" writings of the apostles, there were scores of documents written during the first few centuries of Christianity that weren't included in the canon of scripture—some because they were written too late to be included, and others whose content was highly questionable, or patently heretical, or whose authorship was suspect.

Finally, there were writings by the earliest of the church leaders, including

Clement (died around AD 99), the first-century bishop of Rome, who wrote a letter to the church at Corinth around AD 95. Ignatius (around AD 35 to around 110), a bishop of Antioch in Syria, also sent letters to the Ephesian, Magnasian, Trallian, Roman, Philadelphian, and Smyrnan churches, as well as to Polycarp (around AD 70 to around 155), the Greek bishop of Smyrna.

What to Leave in, What to Leave Out

Though the canon of scripture wasn't officially recognized—at least by any human institution—until the fourth century AD, the early church recognized the authenticity of certain letters and books far earlier than that. During the first few centuries of Christianity, the church had several criteria for recognizing a writing as being truly inspired. Some of these criteria applied to the writers themselves (for example, was the writer recognized as a true prophet of God whose authority was confirmed by the presence of miracles?), and some applied to the writing itself (for example, does the writing tell the absolute truth about God, and without contradiction or deceit?). All of the books the church used and recognized as inspired during those early years met those criteria.

The process of canonizing the New Testament books began during the times of the apostles, some of whom recognized one another's writings as inspired, and therefore scriptural. For example, the apostle Paul quoted the writings of Luke and referred to them as being scripture on a par with the Old Testament (see 1 Timothy 5:18; compare with Luke 10:7). Peter acknowledged that Paul's writings were truly inspired, even likening them to "the rest of the Scriptures" (2 Peter 3:16).

Also, the early believers of that time recognized the writings of the

New Testament apostles and others as scripture. These early Christians immediately recognized the apostles as men divinely appointed and gifted to communicate God's Word to the world around them. That is why the Bible tells us that they "welcomed it not as the word of men, but as it is in truth, the word of God, which also effectively works in you who believe" (1 Thessalonians 2:13), and why they obeyed the apostles' instructions to spread their writings to believers throughout the known world (see Colossians 4:16; 1 Thessalonians 5:27).

The process of acknowledging the canon of New Testament scripture continued during the time of the early church fathers—between the first and third centuries AD Clement, in his writings to various churches, made mention of at least eight books that are included in the New Testament; and Ignatius of Antioch acknowledged seven books. Circa AD 108 Polycarp, a personal disciple of the apostle John, acknowledged fifteen New Testament books. Later, Irenaeus (around 130–200), the bishop of Lyon in Gaul (now France), mentioned twenty-two New Testament books, giving special attention to Paul's epistles, which he wrote about more than two hundred times. Finally, Hippolytus of Rome (around 170 to around 236), one of the most prolific writers in early Christianity, recognized twenty-two.

In those days, efforts were occasionally made to compile a canon of scripture. The first known list of New Testament scripture is called the "Muratorian Canon," which was discovered in the eighteenth century and believed to date to the second century. It included all the New Testament books except Hebrews, James, and 3 John. (During that time, those three books, as well as 2 Peter and 2 John, were not yet universally accepted as scripture.)

Acknowledging What
Is Already the Truth

As the Christian faith began to expand and churches became more established, the rise in false teachers—as well as some Christians' acceptance of those teachers—moved the faithful leaders in the church to realize that they needed to make a stand against those errors and formally acknowledge which writings were truly the inspired Word of God.

By the beginning of the fourth century, most of the books now in the New Testament had long been treated as scripture. But a few books still required further examination and approval before they could be declared a part of the canon.

Around AD 363, approximately thirty Christian leaders from Asia Minor met at the Council of Laodicea. Among the several items on the agenda at this meeting was the formal adoption of the canon of scripture. This council held that only the Old Testament, including the Apocrypha, and the twenty-seven books in the New Testament to this day could be read in the churches. The Council of Hippo in 393 and the Council of Carthage in 397 followed suit, affirming the same twenty-seven books as the New Testament canon.

These councils didn't arbitrarily choose the twenty-seven books that make up the New Testament, and they didn't just choose the ones they liked best. The process of adopting the canon included putting each "questionable" book through a rigorous five-part test to make certain it deserved a place in the Bible. Here is the essence of each of the five questions asked about each book before it was accepted:

Is the book's author a true apostle or closely connected to one or more of the apostles? For example, Matthew and John, both of whom wrote Gospels included in the canon, were in that group of twelve original apostles whom Jesus appointed. Mark and Luke were not among that group, but they both had close relationships with apostles— Mark with the original Twelve during Jesus' earthly ministry and later with the apostle Paul; and Luke with Paul, whom Luke accompanied on his last missionary journey (see chapter 1).

Does the body of Christ at large accept the book as inspired? As pointed out earlier, by the time of the councils of Laodicea, Hippo, and Carthage, the church as a whole had already acknowledged most of the scriptures contained in the New Testament as inspired. These writings were already in wide circulation in the churches and were accepted as the Word of God.

Is the book consistent with accepted Christian doctrine? In chapter 2 we discussed how God, through the centuries, has passionately and jealously guarded His written Word against the many possible human errors. When the councils acknowledged the canon of the New Testament, they did so with a keen eye on the message of those books, thus ensuring that no contradictory teachings or doctrines found their way into the canon.

Does the book's content reflect the high moral and spiritual principles that would reflect a work of the Holy Spirit? Many of the books making the rounds in Christian circles at that time reflected a tolerance or acceptance of either the pagan practices or false teachings of the day. The church leaders at these councils knew those things would never pass muster with the teachings of Christ or of the apostles. Only those books that faithfully reflected the character and standards of Christ Himself and of His apostles were considered for inclusion in the canon.

Missing the Cut. . .
and Why

At the time of the councils that acknowledged the twenty-seven books of the New Testament as part of the canon of scripture, there were countless "Gospels," letters, and other manuscripts making their way around the region. Many of those books were rejected because they were written too late, and many others didn't make it into the Bible because they contained erroneous or heretical teaching, or because their authorship was in question. Here are just a few of the better-known examples of books that didn't make the cut:

The Gospel of Thomas—This book contains 114 sayings attributed to Jesus, some of which resemble some of His sayings in the four Gospels, and some

continued on next page. . .

continued from previous page. . .

of which don't appear in any form in the Gospels or which plainly contradict what is written in them. The early church leaders knew this and deemed this book a forgery, and they rejected it out of hand.

The Gospel of Mary—In this book, Mary Magdalene is portrayed as an apostle who receives special teachings from Jesus. Much of the teaching in this book was patently Gnostic (Gnosticism was a heresy that held, among many other errors, that Jesus Christ was not the divine Son of God), so it found no acceptance from the early church fathers.

The Gospel of Judas—This is a Gnostic gospel that records supposed conversations between Judas Iscariot and Jesus. This "Gospel," contrary to the

continued on next page. . .

continued from previous page. . .

four in the canon of scripture, portrays Judas not as the betrayer of Jesus Christ but as a man who acted purely out of obedience to Christ's stated instructions.

The Apocalypse of Peter—This book, which early church leaders rejected because they doubted its authorship, gives the reader a detailed account of hell, but it also suggests a way out of hell for sinners even after their death. That was problematic for church leaders, because it suggested that people could do whatever they wanted during their lives and still be saved from hell.

The Canon of Scripture—
Who *Really* Decided?

As you've read through this chapter, you've seen some of the events that led to the acceptance of the biblical canon. You've read how what was once a list of countless documents was pared down until it became what we have today: an error-free and contradiction-free Bible that holds perfectly to God's message of salvation for humankind.

How, you may be asking, did such a large number of people—people with the same kinds of flaws and weaknesses we all have today—come to the agreements necessary to produce such a perfect piece of work as the Holy Bible? The answer lies in the guiding hand of God in bringing the process to completion.

All the way through the process of producing the Bible—from the actual writing of the scriptures clear through to the Christian church's recognition of the books God intended to comprise His written Word—you can see the hand of God, working to make sure His message to His people and to a fallen world became exactly what He intended it to be.

No one man or group of men simply *decided* what books would be kept in the canon of scripture and which would be rejected. That happened when God Himself, using the guidance of His Holy Spirit, allowed people to understand which of the books written in the first few centuries of Christianity were truly inspired, or "God-breathed." In other words, the inclusion of the books we have in the Bible today was God's decision and God's work, not man's.

4
Different Languages, Same Message
The Work of Translating the Bible

Down through the centuries, God used gifted and dedicated men to preserve His written Word and keep it true to its original meaning. We can count on the indisputable fact that the message of the Bible has never changed; that it is the same now as it was when first recorded thousands of years ago.

Paraphrasing the prophet Isaiah, the apostle Peter writes, "All flesh is as grass, and all the glory of man as the flower of the grass. The grass withers, and its flower falls away, but the word of the Lord endures forever" (1 Peter 1:24–25). This means that even though people come into and go out of this world, God's commands, promises, and words of encouragement for those who follow Him never change.

What *have* changed, however, are the languages in which God's Word is communicated. Very few people in today's world speak Hebrew or Greek, the languages used to record God's written Word. But God, again using gifted and dedicated men to do His work, has made it possible for people to read and understand the Bible, and to do so in their own languages.

This chapter is dedicated to acknowledging the work of those dedicated souls who committed themselves to making sure the common people could read and understand the Bible. The process started before the birth of Christ, when changes in the language of the Jewish people made it necessary to translate the Hebrew scriptures.

The Septuagint: A Model
of Scripture Translation

Centuries before the birth of Jesus Christ, the Hebrew language was all but dead among the common Jewish people living outside of Palestine (now Israel). Though the highly educated Jewish religious leaders of that time understood the language, most Jewish people spoke Greek. For that reason, it was necessary to translate the Hebrew scriptures into Greek.

The translation of the Hebrew scriptures began around 285 BC. This work was called the Septuagint, a name derived from the Latin word for "seventy." One highly doubtful story held that it took the seventy-two translators seventy-two days to finish their work, but in truth, the project took much longer than that.

The translation of the Septuagint was started in Alexandria on the orders of Egyptian King Ptolemy, who wanted the library of Alexandria to include the wisdom literature of all the world's ancient religions. Ptolemy contacted the Jewish chief priest Eleazar and asked him to send Hebrew scholars from Jerusalem to work on the project. Six were chosen from each of the twelve tribes of Israel, which accounts for the accepted number of seventy-two translators. At first, only the Torah (the first five books of the Old Testament) was translated, but eventually the other books were translated and added to the collection. By the time of the birth of Christ, the Septuagint was the translation of the scriptures most Hellenistic (meaning influenced by the Greek culture of the time) Jews used. It was also the text the early churches—which had no New Testament at the time—read from at their gatherings, as well as the text the apostles quoted when they wrote their epistles to various churches.

In time, what we now call the New Testament was written and compiled in Greek. But nearly four centuries

later, more changes in language necessitated another key development in the
translation of scriptures—both Old
Testament and New.

The Bible in the
"Common Language"

During Jesus' earthly ministry in Palestine, the common language of the
people in that part of the world was
Aramaic. But the four Gospels, as well
as Paul's letters and other New Testament books, were written in Greek. By
late in the fourth century, few people
in the Roman Empire could speak or
read Greek. By that time, the dominant
language in that part of the world was
Latin, and that made it necessary for
the scriptures to be translated into that
language.

Starting early in the third century,
parts of the Bible had been translated
into Latin, but not the entire Bible, and
there were many Latin texts produced,

but with little uniformity. Around AD 382, Pope Damasus I, who wanted the church to have a standard version of the Bible, asked a scholar named Jerome (around AD 347–420) to translate the scriptures in their entirety into a uniform Latin text.

Jerome started by revising the Gospels, using then-available Greek manuscripts. Around the same time, he started translating the Old Testament, using the Septuagint as his source. He completed the translation around AD 400, and his version came to be known as the Vulgate, which means "in the common (or vulgar) language of the people."

Jerome's translation was the standard version of the Bible used in the Christian church from the fourth to the fifteenth centuries. There was little additional translating of the Bible during that time, even though the Christian faith spread to non-Latin speaking people—and even though Latin itself faded out in time as the people's spoken and written language. That is mostly because the Catholic Church, which became the supreme authority over the people's religious lives, wouldn't allow anyone to translate the Bible into the languages of the people.

There was a definite need for additional Bible translations, and it was only through the heroic, and very risky, efforts of a few brave individuals that the Bible began being translated into the people's common languages.

Wycliffe Bucks
the System

John Wycliffe (sometimes spelled Wyclif or Wycliff) was a gifted theologian and scholar born in Yorkshire, England, in the mid-1320s. He attended Oxford University, where he finished a doctorate in theology in 1372. He later served as a professor at the University of Balliol; and as one of the most distinguished theologians of his time, he served as King Richard II's personal chaplain.

Though Wycliffe was a Catholic priest, he was one of the early dissidents in the Catholic Church. His words and actions later earned him the nickname "Morningstar of the Reformation." When he was in his mid-thirties, Wycliffe began to openly reject and preach against much of the church's erroneous preaching and teaching. For example, he rejected the doctrine that church tradition was equal in authority with the Bible, as well as the infallibility of the pope.

Wycliffe believed that the Bible was the literal, inerrant Word of God. He held that the Bible alone, not the church or any other human institution, was the ultimate authority when it came to the practice of the Christian faith. He also believed that each individual believer had the right and the responsibility to read and interpret the scriptures for himself or herself.

The Roman Catholic Church strictly forbade translation of the Bible into the people's common languages of that time. One enemy of Wycliffe's work summed up the church's position this way: "By this translation, the scriptures have become vulgar, and they are more available to lay [people], and even to women who can read, than they were to learned scholars, who have a high intelligence. So the pearl of the Gospel is scattered and trodden underfoot by swine." But Wycliffe wouldn't be swayed, and he replied to the above by saying, "Englishmen learn Christ's law best in English. Moses heard God's law in his own tongue; so did Christ's apostles."

Wycliffe was well aware that preaching and teaching that all believers should have access to the Bible in their own languages put him at odds with the long-held position of the Catholic Church. But he was willing to risk the wrath of the authorities and move ahead with his plans to translate the Bible into English, an endeavor he began with the help of his close personal friend John Purvey.

With a Little Help from His Friends

Though it was long assumed that the first work of translating the Bible into English was Wycliffe's alone, it is now believed that the "Wycliffite" translations were the result of the efforts of Wycliffe and several other men, including Nicholas of Hereford, John Purvey, and perhaps John Trevisa—all friends and followers of Wycliffe.

The translators worked from the Latin Vulgate. They include in their work what is now the accepted canon of scripture (see chapter 3), as well as several noncanonical texts, which the Reformers (leaders of the Protestant movement such as Martin Luther, John

Calvin, and others) later rejected. It is believed that Wycliffe translated the four Gospels himself and that he may have translated the entire New Testament, leaving the translation of the entire Old Testament to his associates after his death.

The work wasn't completed until several years after Wycliffe died of a stroke in 1384. Against the orders of the Catholic Church, Wycliffe's followers —called the Lollards—distributed handwritten copies of the Bible all over England. (This was before the days of the printing press.) Copies of Wycliffe's Bible remained in use for more than a century, until printed Bibles took their place.

Wycliffe was never convicted of heresy for his words or his work (mostly because the church knew that persecuting a man of such popularity in England would likely cause more problems than it could possibly solve), but about thirty years after his death, church authorities had what they thought was the last laugh when they dug up his bones and had them burned and thrown into the Swift River.

Wycliffe's work was just the beginning when it came to Bible translation into English. The Wycliffe Bible had a huge impact on another reformer of the Christian faith, William Tyndale, who took translation of the Bible several more huge steps forward.

William Tyndale: The Father of the English Bible

William Tyndale had everything a young priest needed to take a high and influential position in the Catholic Church. He was fluent in eight languages, and he was proficient in Hebrew and Greek. But Tyndale's true spiritual passion—making it possible for all English-speaking people to read the Bible for themselves—was at great odds with the position the Catholic

Church still held.

Tyndale was born in Gloucestershire, England, around 1494, more than a century after the death of his predecessor, John Wycliffe. Like Wycliffe, Tyndale said and did things he knew would get him in trouble with the Catholic Church.

And they most certainly did.

The story is told about how Tyndale responded angrily to an English bishop who stated that the common people didn't need to read the Bible but only needed to rely on the word of the pope. "I defy the pope and all his laws!" Tyndale shouted. "And, if God spares me, I will one day make the boy that drives the plow in England to know more of the scriptures than the pope does!"

Getting the Ball Rolling

Around 1521, Tyndale left the academic world and joined the household of Sir John Walsh in Little Sodbury Manor, north of Bath, where he found himself stunned and saddened at the lack of scriptural knowledge on the part of most of the bishops he met.

During his time at Little Sodbury Manor, Tyndale began receiving reprimands for the things he'd been saying to and about the Catholic clergy. By the summer of 1523, Tyndale knew it was time to move on, so he traveled to London, where he sought permission and funding from Cuthbert Tunstall, the newly appointed bishop of London, to begin his work of translating the New Testament into English.

Tunstall flatly denied Tyndale's request, and Tyndale's efforts to get permission for his project from other authorities were also fruitless. "Not only was there no room in my lord of London's palace to translate the New Testament, but also that there was no place to do it in all of England," he lamented.

Tyndale was discouraged but not defeated. If he couldn't receive the church's blessing for his work, then he was going to move forward without it. He began his work at the home of Humphrey Monmouth, a London merchant who was sympathetic to his cause. When Tyndale's work came to the attention of the English Catholic bishops, he was forced to depart London for Germany, where, with the financial support of Monmouth and other English merchants, he continued his work in a somewhat safer environment.

You Heard It Here First

You might be aware of the fact that the English language as we use it today is filled with idioms that come directly from the Bible. But what you probably didn't know is that many of those phrases as they appear in scripture came from the pen

continued on next page. . .

---

continued from previous page. . .

of William Tyndale. As Tyndale translated the scriptures from their original languages, he coined the following English phrases, many of which are in common use today:

- let there be light (Genesis 1:3)
- my brother's keeper (Genesis 4:9)
- the salt of the earth (Matthew 5:13)
- the signs of the times (Matthew 16:3)
- the spirit is willing (Matthew 26:41)
- gave up the ghost (Mark 15:37; Luke 23:46; John 19:30; Acts 5:5)
- a law unto themselves (Romans 2:14)
- the powers that be (Romans 13:1)

continued on next page. . .

continued from previous page. . .

- filthy lucre (1 Timothy 3:3, 8; Titus 1:7; 1 Peter 5:2)
- fight the good fight (1 Timothy 6:12)

Tyndale also introduced several new words to the English language—words that are now commonly accepted as scriptural. Those words include *Jehovah* (essentially the English rendering of the Hebrew name of God), *Passover* (the Jewish holiday known in the original Hebrew as *Pesach* or *Pesah*), *atonement* (literally "at one-ment," which means to unite with God and to cover one's sins), and *scapegoat* (the sacrificial animal that, according to Leviticus 16, covers the sins of the people).

When in Germany. . .

By the time Tyndale arrived in Germany, Martin Luther had already begun translating the Bible into the German language. During his exile at the Wartburg Castle following the 1521 Diet of Worms, in which he refused to recant his Protestant beliefs, Luther spent his time translating the New Testament into German, using the original Greek text. Luther found that Greek text in the 1516 printed Greek New Testament of Erasmus of Rotterdam, who had translated the New Testament from Greek to Latin himself because he recognized that the Latin Vulgate had become so corrupted. Luther later published a German Pentateuch in 1523. In the 1530s he published the entire Bible in German.

Tyndale planned to use Erasmus's text as his source. He visited with Luther in 1525, and by the end of that year, he had completed his translation of the New Testament. His translation was vastly superior to Wycliffe's, simply because he worked from the original languages of scripture, whereas Wycliffe had worked from the Vulgate, which contained many errors in translation, and which had become more and more degraded over the centuries.

Tyndale and his associates arranged for the Bibles, which he had printed in the German city of Cologne, to be smuggled into England, where they were met with an enthusiastic response from the people—and with rage on the part of the authorities, including King Henry VIII, Cardinal Wolsey, and Sir Thomas More, all of whom claimed that Tyndale's work contained literally thousands of errors in translation. The authorities bought up as many copies of the translation as they could get their hands on—which, ironically, only further financed Tyndale's work—and burned them. They also made plans to stop Tyndale for good.

A Man without
a Country

William Tyndale had successfully beaten the centuries-old system and helped make an English translation of the Bible somewhat more available to his countrymen, though Bibles in any language were still hard to come by in those days. But his victories came at great personal cost.

With his New Testaments making their way around England and other parts of the world, Tyndale became a marked man. Though he loved England and missed his friends and family there, he knew it wasn't safe to return to his homeland. For nine years he managed to evade the authorities, while at the same time continuing his work of revising his New Testament and beginning to translate the Old Testament.

Tyndale eventually settled in Antwerp, Belgium, where in 1530 his translation of the Pentateuch (the first five books of the Old Testament) was printed. At that time, he planned to translate the remainder of the Old Testament.

But Tyndale didn't live long enough to realize his dream of an English translation of the complete Bible. In May 1535 Henry Phillips, a fellow Englishman who was actually an agent of the pope, befriended Tyndale. One night Phillips lured Tyndale out to the streets of Antwerp, where he was arrested and then taken to a prison cell in the castle of Vilvorde, near Brussels. In August 1536 Tyndale was condemned as a heretic, and on October 6 of that year, he was given a chance to recant. When he refused, he was hanged and his body burned at the stake.

Picking Up Where Tyndale Left Off

Miles Coverdale, the English Bishop of Exeter, and John Rogers, a protestant

English minister, were William Tyndale's faithful allies during the final six years of his life, and they remained faithful to working toward accomplishing his goal of making an English Bible available for the people to read.

After Tyndale's death, Coverdale completed the translation of the Old Testament, and in 1535 he printed the first complete Bible in the English language, the Coverdale Bible. Two years later Rogers printed the second complete English Bible, this one translated directly from Hebrew and Greek and called Matthew's Bible, after "Thomas Matthew," which is thought to be a pseudonym for John Rogers.

In 1539 Thomas Cranmer, Archbishop of Canterbury, employed Coverdale—at the direction of King Henry VIII—to publish what is now known as the Great Bible, due to its huge size (around fourteen inches thick). The Great Bible, which Coverdale himself published, was the first English Bible authorized for public use. In 1541 Henry ordered that a copy of the Great Bible be placed in every parish. Though the English church still held that the "common" people weren't allowed to possess their own copies of the Bible or to read them on their own (under penalty of imprisonment), Coverdale's work brought English Christians a step closer to being allowed to own and read the Bible for themselves.

A Big Step Backward

Though Henry VIII, who broke with the Catholic Church and embraced Protestantism, allowed men such as Coverdale and Rogers to translate the Bible into English, and even sanctioned and financed their work, this newfound freedom didn't last. After Henry's death, King Edward VI took the throne. After Edward's death, Mary Tudor, a devout Catholic, assumed rule in England. "Bloody" Mary wanted to return England to Roman Catholic rule, and she began a wave of persecution against Protestant reformers and Bible translators, including John Rogers and Thomas Cranmer, who were both burned at the stake as heretics in 1555.

During that time, the Protestant Church at Geneva, Switzerland, became a safe haven for exiled English Protestants, including Miles Coverdale. These Protestant exiles wanted to produce a Bible in the English language for their families to read while they were in exile. In 1560, while working under the protection of John Calvin, the leader of the Geneva church, they published the Geneva Bible, a complete translation into English compiled by William Whittingham, Anthony Bilbey, Thomas Sampson, Christopher Goodman, and William Cole.

The Geneva Bible

The Geneva Bible was an important development in efforts to make the Bible readily available to the common English-speaking Christian.

The Geneva Bible influenced the translators of the 1611 King James Version more than any other previous translation. This Bible, which retained more than 90 percent of William Tyndale's English translation, remained more popular than the 1611 King James Version for decades after the KJV was first published.

The Geneva Bible was the first to include chapter and verse references, as well as marginal notes and references, and was therefore the first of what many modern-day Bible readers take for granted: a study Bible. For more than a century, the Geneva

continued on next page. . .

continued from previous page. . .

Bible was the most popular
Bible among English-speaking
believers. At least 144 editions
of this Bible were published
between 1560 and 1644.

The Geneva Bible was also
the Bible of choice for the Puritans and Pilgrims, and it was
the first Bible taken to what
would become America.

Getting the entire Bible printed
in the language of the people required
immense sacrifice on the part of several individuals. But the time would
come when the Catholic Church relaxed its iron-fisted control over the
scriptures—and over who could possess and read them. When that finally
happened, it opened the door for the
best-selling, most-beloved version of
the Bible ever printed: the King James
Version.

5
The Power of the Printing Press
Johannes Gutenberg's Contribution to Bible Distribution

L iving in an age when you can walk into any bookstore and buy one of any number of translations of the Bible (many for under ten dollars), it's hard to imagine a time when a copy of the book wasn't readily available for anyone who wanted to buy one. But from the times of the apostles all the way to the sixteenth-century Protestant Reformation and beyond, that is exactly the situation most Christians faced.

There was a time when the average believer couldn't just go out and purchase his own copy of the Bible (or most any other book, for that matter), simply because there were so few to be had, and because the process of producing books made them unaffordable to the vast majority of people. During the Middle Ages—the time in European history beginning with the end of the Roman Empire in AD 476 and continuing until around the time Columbus discovered the New World in 1492—the only access most people had to the scriptures was at church, where they heard public readings of the Bible. . .and then not even in their own languages, but in Latin. Only the clergy of that time, and others in more privileged classes, had access to the scriptures, or the ability to read and understand them.

In those days, Bibles, and all other books or other written material, had to be hand-copied by scribes—some of the best-educated, highest-paid men of that age—onto vellum, a fine (and extremely expensive) parchment made from the skin of a calf, lamb, or kid goat. Obviously, that prevented the vast majority of people at that time from owning their own Bibles.

So how did we get where we are today from where the people of Europe were back in the Middle Ages? Read on!

A Man Who Made a Difference. . . A *Huge* Difference

Ask most history students who invented the printing press, and they'll readily answer, "Johannes Gutenberg." Though Gutenberg didn't actually *invent* the printing press or conceive of the idea himself—a cruder form of the technology was actually developed in Asia around the fifth century BC— his improvements to the equipment (namely, movable type, the use of metal molds and alloys, a more refined press, and oil-based inks) allowed for the mass production of printed books for the first time in history.

Gutenberg's innovation was, without question, a driving force in revolutionary historic events such as the Protestant Reformation and the Renaissance, simply because a populace that could buy and read books was a self-educated populace. And a populace that had educated itself was a populace that no longer had to take the word of the then-dominant-but-corrupt Catholic Church when it came to matters regarding the Christian faith.

Gutenberg was born in Mainz, Germany, around 1400. He was the son of an upper-class merchant named Friele Gensfleisch zur Laden and his second wife, Else Wyrich. In 1411 an uprising in Mainz against the upper class forced more than one hundred families to flee the city, including the Gutenbergs. Where Johannes spent his next several years isn't certain, but it is believed that he studied at the University of Erfurt.

Outside of the fact that he was

a goldsmith, gem polisher, and glass manufacturer who taught his trades to others, not a lot is known about Gutenberg's early professional life. In 1448 he returned to his hometown of Mainz, where he took out a loan from Arnold Gelthus, his brother-in-law, probably for the purpose of developing his printing press, which he had in operation by 1450. Around that time, Gutenberg took out a large loan from Johann Fust, a wealthy moneylender in Mainz. After that, Fust's future son-in-law, Peter Schöffer, joined Gutenberg in his venture.

Gutenberg was not the first to attempt to design metal type, but he was the first to develop a technique for producing the type in large quantities, a step absolutely essential to making printing with movable type economically viable. For Gutenberg, this meant designing a typeface and producing molds used for making the individual letters and other printing characters.

It also meant developing a metal alloy pliable enough to cast into printing characters but hard and durable enough to use in the actual printing process.

That left Gutenberg with two more steps: developing inks for printing with his new type, and designing a press that could quickly and efficiently transfer the images to paper or other media. In the past, scribes had used water-based inks in their work, but those inks wouldn't stick to metal type, rendering them worthless for Gutenberg's work. For that reason, Gutenberg developed a stickier, oil-based ink. As for the actual press needed to transfer images from type to paper, Gutenberg cleverly adapted the technology already being used for making wine, cheese, and paper.

Gutenberg set up shop at Hof Humbrecht, a property belonging to a distant relative, and began printing lucrative texts, including thousands of "indulgences" for the Catholic Church. (Indulgences were, in a nutshell, printed slips of paper sold by the church for relief of earthly punishment for sin. It was the abuse of indulgences that raised the ire of the young monk Martin Luther, setting off the chain of events that led to the Protestant Reformation.)

Like most great innovators throughout history, Gutenberg had no idea that his invention would so directly lead to such radical changes in the social, economic, political, and religious world climates over the coming centuries, changes that are still taking place today. And though he used his newly developed technology for many different purposes, the one work he is best known for—the one work that defined his contribution to the world in general, and to Christianity in particular—was what has come to be known as the Gutenberg Bible.

All the "Good News"
That's Fit to Print

There's no doubt that the Bible is the most important book ever written, simply because it is God's communication with His people and with a fallen world. But one printed version of the Bible laid the groundwork for events that would give more people the ability to own Bibles and also help make the complete Bible as accessible and affordable as it is today.

The Gutenberg Bible, the first full-length book ever printed on a movable-type printing press, established the superiority of Gutenberg's technology over anything that existed before. And though common ownership of copies of the Bible wouldn't happen in Gutenberg's lifetime—or even very soon after that—it made it possible for a progressively better educated European middle class to afford books, and other reading materials, of their own.

The Gutenberg Bible—also known

as the 42-line Bible (or B42, so-called because almost every two-column page in the work contained forty-two lines of type) or the Mazarin Bible—was Johannes Gutenberg's first major and still best-known work, and it is considered a major factor in the start of the "Gutenberg Revolution" and the "Age of the Printed Book."

Big Money Bibles

Ask any knowledgeable book collector about the most valuable volumes in existence, and he'll mostly likely place the Gutenberg Bible at the top of the list. Of the 180 or so original copies of the work, only 48 are known to still exist, though not all of them are complete. Of the remaining copies, 21 are considered "perfect."

Because copies of the Gutenberg Bible are so rare, and because they represent such an

continued on next page. . .

continued from previous page. . .

important part of history, they are nearly priceless. In 1987 a Japanese book buyer paid $5.4 million to purchase a portion of the Old Testament at Christie's Auction in London. The last sale of a complete Gutenberg Bible took place nine years before that, again at Christie's Auction, and the copy went for $2.2 million.

Today, a complete Gutenberg Bible is valued at an estimated $25–$35 million. Single pages alone fetch around $25,000 each.

The Gutenberg Bible was a 1,286-page printed version of the Latin Vulgate, some of which was printed on vellum and some on paper. It's not certain when Gutenberg conceived the idea for his Bible, but the finished project was no doubt the result of several years' work. Preparation for the project began around 1450, with Gutenberg again receiving the financial backing of Johann Fust.

The exact date the first Bible came off Gutenberg's printing press isn't known for certain, but it is believed that the first finished copies became available in 1454 or 1455. After printing, each copy was illuminated (decorated) and rubricated (supplemented with red text for emphasis) by hand, making each copy of the Gutenberg Bible unique.

The Printing Press Goes "Continental"

Gutenberg's innovation was largely unknown to the world outside of Mainz until 1462, when the troops of Adolph von Nassau, the Archbishop of Mainz, sacked the city following von Nassau's loss to Theodoric of Isenburg-Büdingen in an election for archbishop of the city, the office to which Pope Pius II had appointed von Nassau.

Johann Fust's printing office was burned to the ground, and Gutenberg himself, by now an elderly man, suffered losses in his own business and had to move to Eltville. About four hundred residents of Mainz died in the conflict, and hundreds of others were forced to flee the city, including typographers who took with them the know-how needed to start using printing presses throughout the region.

This "new" invention was a huge hit in Europe, and printing offices were set up in Rome, Paris, Krakow, and Westminster. Compared with the ancient technology of woodblock printing, movable-type printing was faster, more durable, more uniform, and much cheaper. In addition, the use of metal lettering led to the introduction of the use of fonts and other innovations—most of which we now take for granted—in the printing trade.

All of that meant more books printed at less cost, which meant, in time, a better-read middle class in Europe.

Before, written materials could be produced by, at best, the hundreds. But with the advent of Gutenberg's printing press, books and other written materials could be printed and distributed by the tens of thousands. People all over Europe now had easier access to a variety of written materials.

Historians acknowledge that Gutenberg's development of a more practical and efficient printing press had an incalculable impact, first on Europe, and then on the rest of the world. For example, with this new ease of production of printed materials, the writings of Martin Luther—most notably his Ninety-five Theses, which were essentially a challenge to debate many of the corrupt practices of the Catholic Church at that time—found a wider audience all over Europe, giving the Protestant Reformation its steam among the masses.

But as it turned out, the Gutenberg Bible was the first of many versions of the Good Book that found its way to printing presses and into the hands of the European people—and, over the course of time, in their own language.

The Bible in European Tongues

Because the development of the movable-type printing press took place in Germany, it only makes sense that the first "native language" Bibles were published in German.

In 1466, two years before Gutenberg's death, Johannes Mentelin published a German-language Bible—the first printed in any vernacular language—using Gutenberg's printing press. Called the Mentel Bible, it was a literal translation of the Latin Vulgate. The Mentel Bible was printed in Strassburg, and it appeared in at least eighteen editions until Martin Luther's 1522 translation replaced it. In 1467 Adolph Rusch of Ingweiler printed the first Bible in Roman type. In 1469 Conrad Winters de Homborch printed the Cologne Bible, which was likely the first Bible printed in a monastery.

Bible Goofs

Though Gutenberg's development of his printing press led to a huge wave of Bible publishing in Europe, it didn't eliminate human error in the translation and printing processes. Throughout the centuries, printers' mistakes and mistranslations have led to many errors—some of them very serious—in particular translations of the Bible. Here are just a few of many examples:

- In 1561, in the second edition of the Geneva Bible,

continued on next page. . .

---

continued from previous page. . .

an error occurred in Matthew 5:9, which read, "Blessed are the place makers; for they shall be called the children of God." The misprint was corrected to properly read "peace makers."

- In "The Judas Bible," printed in 1611, Matthew 26:36 has Judas, not Jesus, telling the disciples, "Sit ye here while I go yonder and pray," prior to Christ's arrest in the Garden of Gethsemane.

- In "The Sin On Bible," printed in 1716, John 8:11 reads, "Go and sin on more," rather than the correct "Go and sin no more."

continued on next page. . .

continued from previous page. . .

- In the 1763 printing of "The Fool's Bible," Psalm 14:1 reads, "The fool hath said in his heart there is a God," rather than "there is no God."

- Probably the most infamous of these errors appears in "The Wicked Bible" or "Adulterous Bible," printed in 1631, which left the word *not* out of the seventh commandment (Exodus 20:14), leaving it reading, "Thou shalt commit adultery." Only eleven copies of that printing are known to exist today.

But that was just the beginning. In the coming centuries, the Bible was translated into and printed in every European language. As the power structure of the church relaxed—mostly out of necessity—its control over what language scripture could be translated into, printed versions of the Bible in languages other than Latin began appearing all over Europe.

The "common people" could now read the truths of scripture for themselves without having to rely on church authorities. The effects on the political, economic, and spiritual landscape in Western society were enormous.

The Rewards Aren't Always in This Life

You would think that a man who developed a technological advance as important as the printing press would have spent the rest of his life on easy street. But that's far from what happened. From the time Johannes Gutenberg printed his first Bible, a series of events left him broke and struggling to get by for much of the rest of his life.

In 1455, around the time reports of a printed Latin Bible were making their way around Europe, a legal or financial conflict broke out between Gutenberg and Johann Fust, who accused Gutenberg of embezzling the funds Fust had lent him for his work on the printing press and the Bible and demanded back all the money immediately. Fust sued Gutenberg, by now deeply in debt, at the archbishop's court. The court found in favor of Fust, who was awarded control of the Bible printing workshop and half of all the Bibles already printed.

Gutenberg was now, for all practical purposes, bankrupt. He is believed to have started (or restarted) a small printing shop, and is also believed to have taken part in the printing of a Bible in around 1459 in

Bamberg, Germany. Meanwhile, what was now the Fust-Schöffer printing shop published the *Mainz Psalter* of 1457 (a Psalter is a book containing all the psalms of the Bible, as well as other devotional material), which included the printer's name and date and the mechanical process used to print it, but made no mention of Johannes Gutenberg's contributions to the printing of that volume.

Though Gutenberg received little financial benefit from his invention, in 1465 Adolph von Nassau honored his achievements by giving him the title of Hofmann (gentleman of the court). That declaration included a stipend (sort of a salary) for the remainder of his life, an annual court suit, and 2,180 liters of grain and 2,000 liters of wine— all tax-free.

When Gutenberg died in 1468, his contributions to German society were still mostly unknown to the common people. His body was buried in the Franciscan church at Mainz, which was later destroyed. In 1504 Professor Ivo Wittig of Mayence University, in a book he had written, mentioned Gutenberg as the inventor of typography. Wittig also erected a monument in Gutenberg's honor in Mayence. In 1567, nearly a century after Gutenberg's death, the first portrait of him appeared in Heinrich Pantaleon's biography of famous Germans.

Gutenberg's Historic and Spiritual Legacy

No serious historian can leave the name of Johannes Gutenberg off the list of history's most important people. Clearly, Gutenberg's printing press helped pave the way for the Renaissance and the Protestant Reformation, both of which had incalculable effects on the way we live, think, read, and worship today.

Johannes Gutenberg played a key

part in making the Word of God available to all people and all tongues. And while he takes a rightful place in the history of humankind, he also took a vitally important place in God's plans to make His written Word available to every nation and in every tongue.

6

The Rise of the All-Time Bestseller

The King James Version and Other Modern Translations

After the death of Mary Tudor in 1558, her half sister, Elizabeth I, ascended to the throne of England. In 1559 the English Parliament revoked the Catholicism of the previous monarchy. In 1563 what is called the "Elizabethan Settlement" reestablished the Church of England.

With Queen Mary out of the way, the once-exiled English reformers returned to their homeland, where they could now live in relative safety. The Church of England—also known as the Anglican Church—at that time reluctantly tolerated the printing and distribution of the Geneva Bible, even though the marginal notes in the work were vehemently against the institutional church of the day.

Church of England leaders wanted a new version of the Bible, one without what they considered inflammatory marginal notes. Under Elizabeth I, the Great Bible was again placed in the churches. In 1568 a revision of the Great Bible—called the Bishop's Bible, which church leaders considered a more literal translation than the Great Bible—was printed and distributed. Nineteen editions of the Bishop's Bible, which has been referred to as "the rough draft of the King James Version," made it to print between 1568 and 1606, but none of them were popular with the people.

In 1582 the Catholic Church in England, more than anything seeing the futility of clinging to the centuries-long Latin-only law of Bible translation, particularly in a Protestant nation, changed its tune and allowed the printing of Bibles in English, and even printed an official Roman Catholic English Bible. Using the badly distorted Vulgate as its source, the church published an English Bible that had been translated in a Catholic college in the city of Rheims: the Rheims New Testament. Later, in 1609, the Catholic Church published the Douay Old Testament, which was translated at a college in the city of Douay. The two were later combined, producing a Bible called the Douay-Rheims Version.

Though the English Protestants had it far better under Elizabeth than they had under Mary Tudor, there was an undercurrent of conflict, namely between more traditional Anglicans and more radical Protestants who came to be known as "Puritans."

The conflicts between the Church of England and the Puritans continued through the reign of Elizabeth's successor, King James I, and they played an important part in another pivotal moment in the history of Bible translation.

It was a part King James himself is most remembered for to this day.

A "Crowning" Achievement

King James I (born on June 19, 1566, as James Charles Stuart) was the son of Mary Queen of Scots and Lord Darnley, who was murdered before James's first birthday. Crowned at one year of age, James served as king of Scotland (as James VI) for thirty-six years before ascending to the throne of England in 1603, after the death of Elizabeth I.

James I accomplished his lifelong dream of uniting England, Scotland, and Ireland into what he called "Great Britain." But he began his reign during a time of some long-festering religious conflicts in his kingdom, which he attempted to resolve when he called the Hampton Court Conference in mid-January 1604.

At the conference, English Christian leaders were allowed to air their differences and present what they believed were problems within English Christianity. One of those leaders was John Reynolds, the president of Corpus Christi College in Oxford and a Puritan, who told the court that a new and improved translation of the Bible into English was needed—one free of marginal notes (like those in the Geneva Bible) and one that held absolutely true to the original languages of scripture.

King James's Passion for the Bible

Though there is debate about the personal lifestyle of King James I, there can be no doubt that he had an inner passion for the Word of God, which he demonstrated in this excerpt from a letter to his eldest son, Prince Henry: "Diligently read His Word, and earnestly pray for the right understanding thereof. Search the scriptures, saith Christ, for

continued on next page. . .

continued from previous page. . .

they will bear testimony of Me. The whole scriptures, saith Paul, are profitable to teach, to improve, to correct, and to instruct in righteousness, that the man of God may be perfect unto all good works."

James I also believed in "the divine right of kings," which held that a monarch received his right to rule directly from God, and it was his own responsibility to rule according to the principles of the Bible, while making sure he paid attention to the good of his subjects.

One of the reasons King James favored a new and updated translation of the Bible was that he objected to the marginal notes in the Geneva Bible, many of which he saw as bordering on disloyalty to the throne.

Although the Bible hadn't been

placed on the court's official agenda, James I listened to and agreed with Reynolds, and he wasted little time in getting started on what would become the best-selling book of all time.

Men at Work—*Hard* Work!

By July 1604 James I had appointed fifty-four of the world's most-renowned Bible scholars and linguists of the day to translate the Bible. Each had a solid grasp on the Hebrew, Greek, and Aramaic languages, and each had written, translated, and edited works in Greek. And each, most importantly, was a Christian man with a passion for the Word of God.

Though fifty-four men were appointed to the task, just forty-seven of them are known to have actually taken part in the work. The translators were divided into six groups—two working at Oxford, two at Cambridge, and two at Westminster—with each group taking responsibility for one section of scripture. They translated from the best Greek and Hebrew manuscripts available at the time, and they also made use of commentaries and earlier English translations. As they worked, they held to fifteen rules for translation, all of which were laid out to ensure that the finished product was an absolutely literal translation from the Hebrew and Greek of the original scriptures into English.

It was painstaking work, completed over a period of several years. Each individual in a group translated the same portion of scripture, and then went over it again until he was satisfied that it was faithful to the original meaning and wording. He then submitted his portion to the rest of his group, which discussed it and decided which translation was the best. When a particular book of the Bible was completed, it was then submitted to the other groups to be examined again. Questions one group had about a particular point were then sent back to the group responsible for the translation. Any disagreements on the text were settled at a meeting of the leaders of each group.

The work, which came to be known as the King James Version, or the Authorized Version, was completed and issued in 1611, with a complete title page reading:

> The HOLY BIBLE, Conteyning the Old Testament, and the New: Newly Translated out of the Original tongues: & with the former Translations diligently compared and revised, by his Majesties Special Commandment. Appointed to be read in Churches. Imprinted at London by Robert Barker, Printer to the Kings most Excellent Majestie. Anno Dom. 1611.

In time, the Authorized Version (called that even though there is no record of it being authorized by anyone in power) of the Bible would take its place as the most loved and influential piece of literature of all time. To this day, it remains the world's best-selling book, and it is still praised for its accuracy in holding to the original Bible manuscripts and for its literary qualities.

The Authorized Version
Takes Its Place

It wasn't long before the King James Version (KJV) replaced the Great Bible as the version used in church parishes throughout England. In Scotland, churches still used the Geneva Bible until 1633, when a Scottish edition of the Authorized Version was printed, and it soon took the Geneva Bible's place in the churches.

The general public was slower to accept the KJV, favoring the Geneva Bible for a few decades after the first printing of the KJV. Large numbers of the Geneva Bible found their way into England from Amsterdam, where printing of the "outdated" Bibles continued until around 1644. The printing of the Geneva editions slowed and then ceased in England after 1616, and in 1633 Archbishop Laud of Canterbury prohibited both their printing and their importation. By the end of the seventeenth century, the KJV had become the only current version of the Bible circulating among English-speaking people.

Over time, the King James Version went through some revisions of its own, including those done in the seventeenth and eighteenth centuries to correct printing errors, which were oftentimes the result of carelessness in the publishing process (see examples in chapter 5). Two editions completed in Cambridge—in 1629 and 1638—attempted to restore the original text and also introduced more than two hundred revisions of the original translators' work.

By the end of the eighteenth century, the Authorized Version was, for all practical purposes, the only Bible used in English-speaking Protestant churches. In 1752 the Catholic Church in England printed a revision of the Douay-Rheims Version that was very close in content to the Authorized Version. The KJV also took the Vulgate's place as the Bible that English-speaking scholars and church leaders used for their work.

Along with Johannes Gutenberg's development of the printing press, the translation of the King James Version remains one of the pivotal developments in the history of Bible translation and publication. But work on "updating" the Bible didn't stop with the KJV. Though the Authorized Version maintained its place as the best-selling Bible of all time, over the four centuries since its completion, the work of making the Bible readable to more people has continued, resulting in a wide variety of translations of God's Word into our spoken language.

Picking Up Where
the KJV Left Off

All you have to do to understand that the English language has changed over the centuries is crack open a copy of the King James Version and start reading. Though the content and meaning of the Bible text are the same as they were when they were written, changes in how we speak and read necessitated changes in how God's Word is presented.

Beginning in 1881, a group of English and American scholars created a new translation called the Revised Version (or English Revised Version), which was intended as a revision of the King James Version, adapting the Bible text to updated English usage.

At the time of the publication of the entire Revised Version in 1885, the King James Version was still the best English Bible translation—both in terms of accuracy and style. The RV translation included elements not seen in the KJV, including arrangement of the text into paragraphs, printing of Old Testament poetry (such as the Psalms) in indented poetic lines, and the addition of marginal notes to point out to the reader variations in wording in ancient manuscripts. For these reasons, the RV is considered the forerunner of all modern Bible translations.

In 1900 Thomas Nelson & Sons, an American publishing company, released the American Standard Version (ASV) Old Testament, and the following year the publishing company published the complete ASV Bible. The work on the ASV began in 1872, with thirty American and British scholars, chosen by the Swiss theologian Philip Schaff, doing their work using much of the work already done on the Revised Version. One of the most notable differences between the Revised Version and the ASV is that the latter uses a more Americanized style of the English language.

The ASV became the basis of four twentieth-century revisions of the Bible:

the Revised Standard Version (released in 1952), the Amplified Bible (1965), the New American Standard Bible (1971), and the Recovery Version (1999). It was also the basis for a popular paraphrase called The Living Bible (1971).

The Bible in the Twentieth and Twenty-first Centuries

The translation of the Bible into more updated English continued throughout the twentieth century and continues to this day, with several versions introduced since the early 1950s.

Below are some of the more popular versions published since the beginning of the twentieth century:

The Revised Standard Version (RSV)—Printed in its entirety in 1952 (the New Testament was published in 1946), the RSV was a comprehensive revision of the KJV, the RV, and the ASV. The RSV, which aimed to be a more readable but still accurate English translation of the original Bible texts, posed the first serious challenge to the popularity of the KJV.

The Amplified Bible (1965)—The first Bible project of the Lockman Foundation, this translation helps the reader understand what scripture really says and really means by taking into account both word meaning and context. This is accomplished by the use of synonyms and definitions in order to "amplify" the meaning of Bible texts.

New American Standard Bible (NASB)—Like so many Bible translations before and since, the purpose of the NASB, which was published in its entirety in 1971, was to update the grammar and terminology of scripture while at the same time staying true to the original texts. Scholars worked for ten years translating from the best available Bible texts.

The Living Bible (TLB)—American author Kenneth N. Taylor was once quoted as saying that he paraphrased the American Standard Version of the Bible in order to make the Bible readable and understandable to the average reader, including children, which he said were his inspiration for his work. The result was The Living Bible, which was released in 1971. Billy Graham used portions of The Living Bible in his evangelistic crusades. This version was the best-selling Bible in the United States in the early 1970s.

Today's English Version (TEV), or Good News Bible (GNB)—The American Bible Society first published the New Testament of this version, titled *Good News for Modern Man*, in 1966, with American and British editions of the complete Bible following in 1976. Working to provide a faithful translation of the original texts into clear, concise, modern English, a committee of Bible scholars translated the original texts they had available into this version.

New International Version (NIV)— This version was conceived in 1965, when years of study by committees from the Christian Reformed Church and the National Association of Evangelicals, an international, trans-denominational group of scholars, concluded that a new translation into contemporary English was needed. The NIV was a result of the work of more than one hundred scholars working from the best available Hebrew, Aramaic, and Greek texts. The NIV New Testament was released in 1973, with the complete NIV Bible following in 1978.

New King James Version (NKJV)— In 1975 Thomas Nelson Publishers commissioned the work for the NKJV, which was intended to be a Bible with the exact content of the KJV, only with updated language (for example, old English pronouns such as "thou," "thee," "ye," and "thine" were changed to reflect modern English). One hundred thirty respected Bible scholars, church leaders, and others worked seven years to complete this project, which was published in its entirety in 1982, three years after the release of the NKJV New Testament.

New Living Translation (NLT)—The NLT is the result of what started out as an effort to revise The Living Bible, but it evolved into an altogether new translation of the Bible. Beginning in 1989, a team of eighty-seven translators began working on the NLT, and the work was completed and published in 1996.

The Message (MSG)—The pastor, scholar, and writer Eugene H. Peterson created The Message: The Bible in Contemporary Language to help people in his Bible study classes better connect with the vital, life-changing message of the Bible. The Message is a paraphrase of the original languages of the Bible, not a literal word-for-word translation. Navpress Publishers began publishing segments of The Message Bible in 1993, and the complete Bible became available in 2002.

Holman Christian Standard Bible (HCSB)—In 2004 Holman Bible Publishers released the HCSB, which is a version of the Bible using both dynamic and formal equivalence, meaning some of the text is translated word for word, while some of it is translated with the goal of conveying the actual thought behind the words.

Different Approaches to Bible Translation

With so many translations or versions of the Bible available today, the natural question that arises is this: Why do they all say essentially the same thing, yet read so differently? That's simply because the translators who produced these Bibles used different approaches to rendering God's Word into English.

The formal equivalence, or *literal*, approach to Bible translation means to translate the text word for word, sometimes at the expense of a word's or phrase's original meaning or

continued on next page. . .

---

continued from previous page. . .

intent. The King James Version, the English Standard Version, and the New American Standard Bible are all examples of Bibles that were translated using formal equivalence.

The *dynamic equivalence* (also called *functional equivalence*) approach to translation emphasizes the *thought* expressed in the original Bible texts over the literalness, word order, and grammar used in those texts—in other words, what the original text *means* over what it says word for word. Many of the more modern translations use *dynamic equivalence*, including the New Living Translation and Today's English Version.

Some Bible translations are examples of the use of both *formal equivalence* and *dynamic equivalence* in translation. Examples of those are the New

continued on next page. . .

continued from previous page. . .
International Version (as well as Today's New International Version), and the New Revised Standard Version.

Finally, there is the *paraphrase*, which technically isn't a translation. To paraphrase means to say the same thing using different words. The best-known of the paraphrased versions of the Bible are The Living Bible and *The Message*.

Which is the Best of the Best?

With all these Bible translations and paraphrases so readily available, the question that so often arises is this: Which one is best?

Which translation or version most faithfully represents the true original message of scripture is a source of constant debate among spiritual leaders as well as Bible scholars. Some hold that most of the versions listed in the previous section, as well as the King James Version itself, are all solid works that faithfully communicate the intended message of the original scriptures. Others hold a narrower view, stating that the KJV and a few others are the only truly accurate renderings of the original. Still others hold the even narrower view that the KJV is the only translation that is absolutely true to the original manuscripts.

The bottom line is that there are several excellent versions of the Bible available, and which one you choose for your personal reading and studies should depend on two important factors. First, which version do you find easier to follow and understand? You will find your Bible reading much more fruitful when you can follow the language used well enough to fully grasp what it is saying to you. Second, when you go shopping for a Bible, begin by praying and asking God to guide you to the version that is best for you. As with anything else in your life of faith, God knows better than anyone what you really need, and that includes which version of the Bible you should be reading.

A Final Note

No book about the Bible would be complete without encouraging you to read the Bible, study the Bible, memorize the Bible, and meditate on the Bible.

You've just finished reading six chapters that give you a brief look at the God-ordained historical events He used to give us the Bible. If when you started reading this book, you somehow knew that God had given you the Bible, you now have a basic understanding of how He did it.

But the purpose in writing this book isn't *just* to give readers a quick rundown of how God gave us the greatest book ever written. While it is certainly valuable to understand exactly how we got the Bible we have today, that bit of knowledge means little if your appreciation for all God has done to give it to you doesn't move you toward a more serious and faithful approach to God's written Word. Though there are certainly blessings in understanding how we got the Bible in the first place, there are even bigger and better ones in focusing your energies on the Bible itself.

Here is a quick overview of what it means to read, study, memorize, and meditate on the Bible:

1. Read the Bible—That sounds pretty basic, but in truth, few Christians have taken the time to simply read the Bible cover to cover. Many study Bibles include year-long schedules for reading through the Bible. One of the benefits of reading the Bible this way is that you get a great overview of the complete story it has to tell.

2. Study the Bible—You can take your Bible reading up several levels when you invest the time and energy to study the Bible. There are several methods for studying the Bible, and all of them can be of great benefit in your walk of faith. There is the deductive study (picking a specific topic and then going through the Bible to find passages that address it); inductive study (studying a particular passage until you understand what it says and what it means); character, event, and place study (self-explanatory); and word study (studying a particular keyword in scripture, as well as its synonyms, to find out what that word means in the biblical context).

Whether you study the Bible in a personal setting or within a group, it's helpful to have some basic tools at the ready—a study Bible, a concordance, a Bible dictionary, and a reliable Bible commentary, as well as a writing utensil and pad to record what you've learned.

3. Memorize the Bible—The apostle Peter instructed believers to "always be ready to give a defense to everyone who asks you a reason for the hope that is in you" (1 Peter 3:15). The best way to follow that important bit of instruction is to commit portions of the Bible to memory. There are many methods of memorizing scripture, but the important part of this process for you is to find a version of the Bible that works best for you, then to read and reread the verse or passage you want to memorize, then write it down and read it aloud. If you have a memorization partner, read the verse to your partner and have him or her do the same for you. Also, don't try to memorize too much at one time! There are those rare individuals with photographic memories, but for the rest of us, it's best to approach scripture memorization in smaller bits.

4. Meditate on the Bible—There's something about the word *meditation* that raises the eyebrows of a lot of Bible-believing Christians. However, the Bible clearly teaches that there is great blessing and power in meditating on God's Word: "Blessed is the man who walks not in the counsel of the ungodly, nor stands in the path of sinners, nor sits in the seat of the scornful; but his delight is in the law of the LORD, and in His law he meditates day and night" (Psalm 1:1–2).

To meditate on something can mean a lot of things, but in this context it means to think deeply about it, to ponder it and consider what it means to you, and, most importantly, to dwell on what the book's Author is saying to you personally.

The Bible is no ordinary book; it is the result of the mouth of God speaking and the hand of God orchestrating events as only He can—simply so that He could give us His written Word to guide our thoughts, our words, and our actions, so that all we think, say, or do pleases Him. Knowing both what God has done to give us the Bible *and* what applying the principles, commands, and promises of the Bible can do for our walk of faith should motivate every believer to make it a central part of his or her life of faith in Jesus Christ.

If you enjoyed

HOW DID WE GET the BIBLE?

be sure to look for these other great Bible resources from Barbour Publishing!

The Complete Guide to the Bible
7" x 9½", Paperback, 512 pages, $19.97
ISBN 978-1-59789-374-9

500 Questions & Answers from the Bible
6" x 9", paperback, 256 pages, $9.97
ISBN 978-1-59789-473-9

Bible Atlas & Companion
8" x 10", paperback, 176 pages, $9.97
ISBN 978-1-59789-779-2

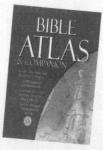

Available wherever Christian books are sold.